Date

Dear

From

Special Blessings For You Today

Designed by Christian Art Gifts

Printed in China

ISBN 1-86920-328-3

03 04 05 06 07 08 09 10 11 12 – 10 9 8 7 6 5 4 3 2 1

Special Blessings For You Today

Karla Dornacher

christian art gifts

This is the day the LORD has made;
welcome
we will rejoice and be glad in it!

PSALM 118:24, NKJV

JUST FOR TODAY . . .
I will not look back.

I'm a new creation,
the old me is gone
and this is a new path
I'm walking on.

Today is a new day,
with hope for tomorrow
and I'm not looking back
with regret or with sorrow.

For my sins are forgiven,
I'm washed white as snow
and I've said, Lord, send me
where You want me to go.

So He's filled me with love
to finish out the race
until the day of glory
when I'll see Him face to face.

Just for today...

I will drink in the joy of the Lord.

A merry heart does good, like medicine.

Proverbs 17:22, NKJV

Laugh out loud.
Seize the silly.
Laugh at yourself.
Tickle me funny.
Lighten up.
Hunt for humor.
Cheer the weary.
Be the jester.

Let God fill your heart with laughter.

JUST FOR TODAY...
I will open my life to God.

Open your mouth wide,
and I will fill it.

Psalm 81:10, NKJV

A baby bird makes no effort
to look for its own provision.
It simply follows its mama around,
with mouth open wide,
waiting expectantly to be filled.

Only God can fill our deepest
needs, desires and longings.
He waits for us to open wide
so He can fill us
with His glory, goodness and grace.

Whatever things are true,
whatever things are noble,
whatever things are just,
whatever things are pure,
whatever things are lovely,
whatever things are of good report,
if there is any virtue
and if there is anything praiseworthy ~
meditate on these things.

Philippians 4:8

JUST FOR TODAY...

I will think on these things.

JUST FOR TODAY...

I will sow seeds of
kindness into the lives
of those around me.

Plant a few
Kingdom Seeds today
by smiling and showing kindness
to three people you don't know.
Let them see Jesus in you
and through you.

Remember God smiles at you too!

Pansies
Kingdom Seeds
of
Remembrance

Just for today...
I will love someone
in a tangible, touchable way.

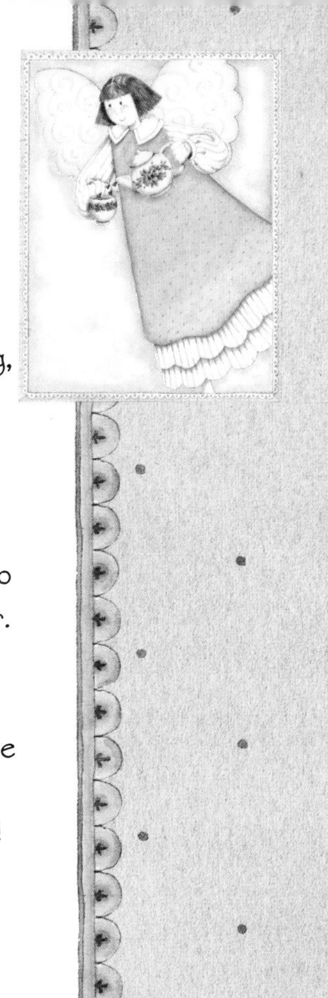

Give an apple pie with a note saying,
"You are the apple of God's eye."

Write an anonymous note
to someone you appreciate
and include a gift certificate for two
to a restaurant or the movie theater.

When paying for your food at a
drive~through restaurant, pay for the
folks two cars behind you.
They'll never figure out it was you!

My little children, let us
not love in word or in tongue,
but in deed and in truth.

1 John 3:18, NKJV

Savored Moments

JUST FOR TODAY...

I will count my blessings
and name them one by one.

The LORD bless you and keep you;
the LORD make His face shine upon you,
and be gracious to you.

Numbers 6:24~25

An attitude of gratitude
will chase the blues away.
Consider all God's done for you
and let Him hear you say ~
Thank You Father, for this moment,
open my eyes that I may see.
Forgive me for all I take for granted ~
Your love and blessings
that flow so free.

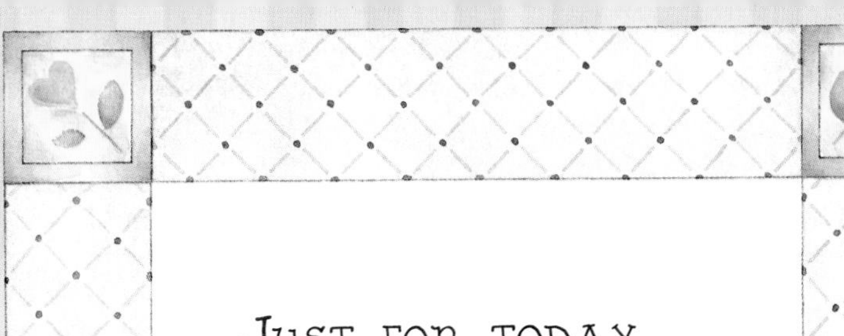

JUST FOR TODAY...
I will dream big dreams.

Where there's no vision,
the people perish.

Proverbs 29:18, KJV

God gave you an imagination.
It's the vehicle of all creation.
It leads to your edification
when you use it for
God's glorification.

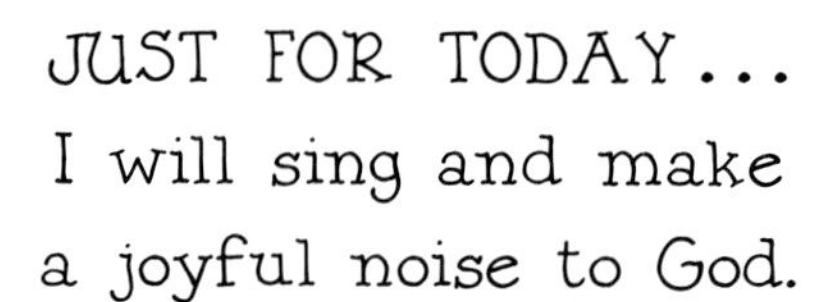

JUST FOR TODAY...
I will sing and make
a joyful noise to God.

Turn on the music
and sing along.
Praise the Lord
with a joyful song.
Lift up your voice
and bless His name.
Declare His glory
and His fame.

"Oh, sing to the Lord a new song!"
God lives here

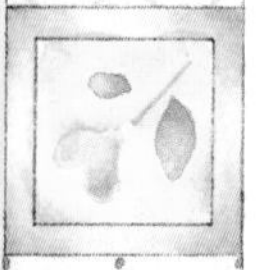

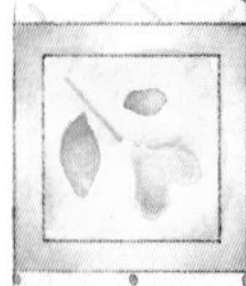

GOD SHALL SUPPLY
ALL YOUR NEEDS

JUST FOR TODAY...

I will trust in God's provision.

Birds don't worry about their needs being met. They trust in God's provision. The Lord says you are more valuable to Him than many sparrows.

As you trust God,
He will meet all your needs
according to His riches in glory ...
it's His promise!

Refresh My Heart
Cloth
Promises
Psalm 119:105
Psalm 119

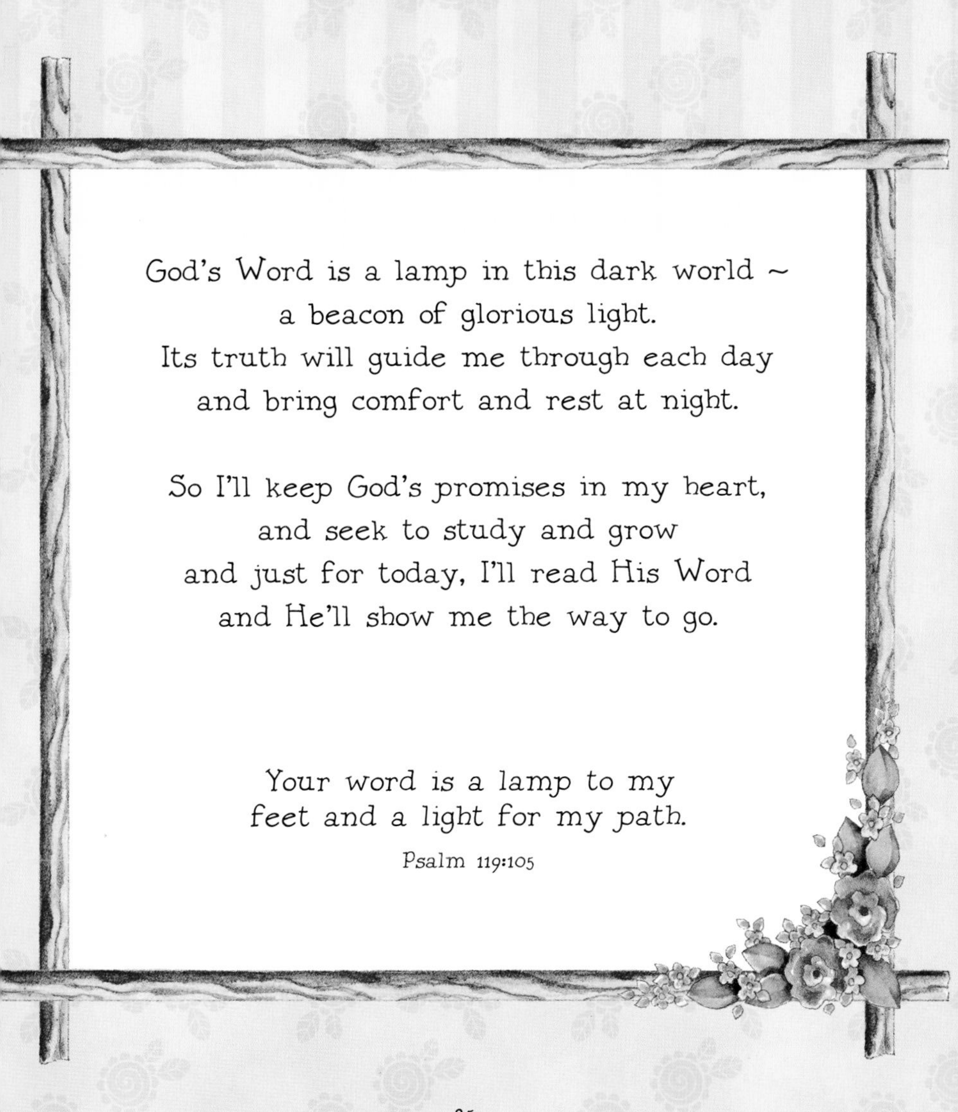

God's Word is a lamp in this dark world ~
a beacon of glorious light.
Its truth will guide me through each day
and bring comfort and rest at night.

So I'll keep God's promises in my heart,
and seek to study and grow
and just for today, I'll read His Word
and He'll show me the way to go.

Your word is a lamp to my
feet and a light for my path.

Psalm 119:105

Holy Bible

Just for today...

I will hide God's Word in my heart.

I have hidden Your word in my heart
that I might not sin against You.

Psalm 119:11

Just for Today...

I will not forget the benefits of
knowing God:

Unconditional love.
Forgiveness of sins.
Eternal salvation.
A second chance.
Peace beyond understanding.
Truth that sets me free.
Protection from the evil one.
My daily bread.
The joy of the Lord.
And so much more.

Forget not all His benefits

Forget-Me-Not

Seeds of Praise

Psalm 103:2

Let everything that has breath praise the Lord
Psalm 150:6
Amazing Grace
Holy Bible
Psalms
Promises

Like true love, praise is not
based on emotion,
but on a decision.
Your feelings may say
there is nothing to be thankful for,
but look around ~
God's love surrounds you.

Focus on what is true, good,
and worthy of praise,
and your thoughts and attitudes
will be transformed.

So JUST FOR TODAY...
praise the Lord!

Rejoice in the

JUST FOR TODAY...

I will rejoice ~
not because of my
circumstances ~
but because of my God.

"Let all those rejoice
who put their trust in You;
let them ever shout for joy,
because You defend them;
let those also
who love Your name
be joyful in You.
For You, O LORD,
will bless the righteous;
with favor
You will surround him
as with a shield."

Psalm 5:11~12, NKJV

Come to Me
all you
who are weary
and burdened,
and I
will give you rest.
Matthew 11:28
You are invited

My friend,

Jesus has sent you a personal invitation to come into His presence, to sit with Him in a quiet place, and find rest and peace for your soul.

JUST FOR TODAY...

accept His invitation.

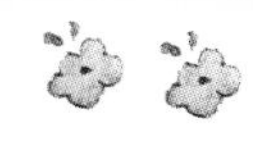

Just for today...

I will look at life
with faith for the present,
hope for tomorrow,
and a love and longing
for eternity.

He leads me
beside quiet waters.
Psalm 23:2

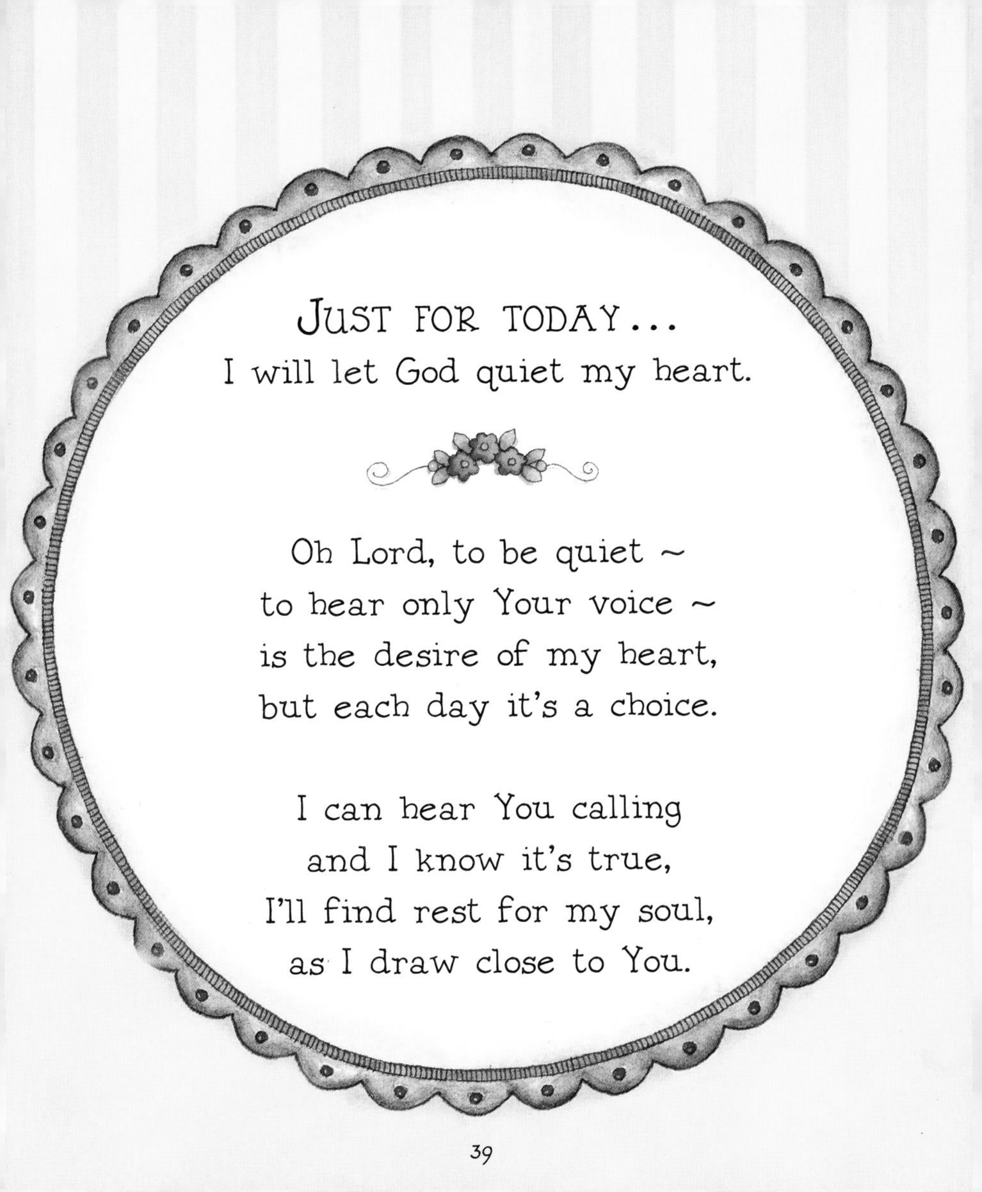

Just for today...

I will let God quiet my heart.

Oh Lord, to be quiet ~
to hear only Your voice ~
is the desire of my heart,
but each day it's a choice.

I can hear You calling
and I know it's true,
I'll find rest for my soul,
as I draw close to You.

Rose of Sharon
Lily of the Valley
Morning Star
Heavenly Seed Catalog
Gardener's Journal
sow faith,
reap
blessing

JUST FOR TODAY...

I will believe that
God is bigger than
all my problems.

"Nothing is
impossible with God."
Luke 1:37

Weeds to Clean Out
WORRY
PRIDE
JEALOUSY
BUSYNESS
FEAR
COMPLACENCY
GREED
ANGER
SELF-PITY
GOSSIP
BUSYBODY
LUST
LAZINESS

Trust in the Lord with all your heart,
and lean not on your own understanding;
in all your ways acknowledge Him,
and He shall direct your paths.
Proverbs 3:5~6, NKJV
REST
RETREAT
BLESSING
JOY

I will let go and let God.

There is a path
that we're called to walk on,
but it requires holding onto God's hand.
So you'll have to let go
of the struggles you're carrying,
and let Jesus lead you as only He can.

The path before you
is topsy and turvy,
with mountaintops high
and valleys so low,
so lean only on God;
not your own understanding,
and you can trust Him to never let go.

COME, LET US REJOICE
Celebrate Life
Psalm 66:6

JUST FOR TODAY...

I will celebrate life!

I want to fill my life today
with the spirit of celebration.
I want to applaud each new day
and give it a standing ovation.

For yesterday has come and gone,
and tomorrow has yet to arrive.
But today is a moment of eternity
and I'm thankful I'm alive.

Lord, help me not to take for granted
all Your blessings great and small.
Open my heart to celebrate,
to embrace and enjoy them all.

JUST FOR TODAY...

I will look for God's blessings.

Look for the Lord,
He's all around,
though He may not
make a sound.
His presence can
be most profound
when in the small things
He is found.

You prepare a feast for me
in the presence of my enemies.
You welcome me as a guest,
anointing my head with oil.
My cup overflows with blessings.

Psalm 23:5, NLT

Praying one cup of
blessing on top of another...
and another... and another!